Please Take Jake!

amicus readers

by Marie Powell

illustrated by Amy Cartwright

Ideas for Parents and Teachers

Amicus Readers let children practice reading at early reading levels. Familiar words and concepts with close illustration-text matches support early readers.

Before Reading

- Discuss the cover illustration with the child. What does it tell him?
- Ask the child to predict what she will learn in the book.

Read the Book

- "Walk" through the book and look at the illustrations. Let the child ask questions.
- Point out the colored words. Ask the child what is the same about them (spelling, ending sound).
- Read the book to the child, or have the child read to you.

After Reading

- Use the word family list at the end of the book to review the text.
- Prompt the child to make connections. Ask: *What other words end with -ake?*

Amicus Readers are published by Amicus
P.O. Box 1329, Mankato, MN 56002
www.amicuspublishing.us

Illustrations by Amy Cartwright

Produced for Amicus by The Peterson Publishing Company and Red Line Editorial.

Editor Jenna Gleisner
Designer Craig Hinton
Printed in the United States of America
Mankato, MN
2-2014
PA10001
10 9 8 7 6 5 4 3 2 1

Library of Congress Cataloging-in-Publication Data
Powell, Marie, 1958-
  Please take Jake! / Marie Powell.
    pages cm. -- (Word families)
  K to Grade 3.
  Audience: Age 6
  ISBN 978-1-60753-583-6 (hardcover) --
  ISBN 978-1-60753-649-9 (pdf ebook)
  1. Reading--Phonetic method. 2. Reading (Primary) I. Title.
  LB1573.3.P6955 2014
  372.465--dc23
                    2013044008

My name is Blake. This is my little brother Jake. I have to take Jake along everywhere I go.

I go to Grandma's house to **bake** a **cake**. I want to go alone. But I have to **take Jake**.

5

I ask Dad if I can go with him to the lake.

"Sure," he says. "We will also take Jake."

Mom and Dad **take** us to the zoo.

"Can I go see the **snake**?" I ask.

"Sure," Mom says. "Please **take** Jake."

ZOO

HIPPOS >

< SNAKE SHACK

< MONKEYS

I race my bike to the park before Mom can make me take Jake.

"Slow down!" Mom says.

"Please wait for Jake."

I help Mom make my lunch.
I tell her I want to walk
alone to school. But I see
her shake her head.

"Tomorrow Jake will wake up and go with you," Mom says. "You get to take Jake along for his first day of school!"

Word Family: -ake

Word families are groups of words that rhyme and are spelled the same.

Here are the -ake words in this book:

bake	make
Blake	shake
cake	snake
Jake	take
lake	wake

Can you spell any other words with -ake?